What Is It To Be A Lawyer?

Elmer Bragg Adams

In the interest of creating a more extensive selection of rare historical book reprints, we have chosen to reproduce this title even though it may possibly have occasional imperfections such as missing and blurred pages, missing text, poor pictures, markings, dark backgrounds and other reproduction issues beyond our control. Because this work is culturally important, we have made it available as a part of our commitment to protecting, preserving and promoting the world's literature. Thank you for your understanding.

WHAT IS IT TO BE A LAWYER?

AN ADDRESS

BY

HONORABLE ELMER B. ADAMS,

UNITED STATES CIRCUIT JUDGE.

BEFORE THE FACULTY AND STUDENTS
OF THE ST. LOUIS UNIVERSITY
INSTITUTE OF LAW,
JANUARY 26th, 1911,

WHAT IS IT TO BE A LAWYER?

At the outset I wish to acknowledge the great honor and pleasure I have in accepting the kind invitation of your worthy dean to address you this evening. His zeal in behalf of this law school is well known and in most ways highly commendable, but when it takes the turn of securing a dry old lecture from a dry old lecturer who has not been in active participation in the world's recent momentous and startling activities, he seems to me to expose his zeal to a serious criticism. Be this, however, as it may, he must now take the consequences of his act.

Some over forty years ago I was a student in the Harvard Law School. Its interesting curriculum of study, its illustrious professors, its intellectual atmosphere, highly charged with the intense aspirations of the boys, all interested me very much. They had a certain glamour and consequence about them which, while very attractive, were not fully appreciated by me at the time, neither were their advantages understood. Such, I apprehend, is the case with you. You are students of the law in a great university; under wise and learned instructors, and you feel the tingle of noble aspirations and brilliant expectations, but I fear you do not realize the full import of what you are doing. To what end are you here? What is it to be a lawyer? What are its privileges, duties and responsibilities? These are pertinent and grave questions upon which young aspirants for professional honors and rewards should deeply ponder. Illustrious men of high character and learning have guided the destinies of this nation from its beginning, and in all its crises, the lawyer has stood forth as its chief champion and defender. Before the Revolution, when our jurisprudence was in its infancy, Henry, Pendleton, Mason, Otis, Quincy, Adams and others learned in the law largely created and gave direction to public sentiment. They inspired that patriotism which culminated in the Declaration of Independence, the War of the Revolution and our ultimate independent national existence.

The Constitution of the United States, the Ordinance of 1887 and the Judiciary Act of 1889, the corner stones of our national structure, were the result of their learning, wisdom and practical sense.

Later, John Jay, John Rutledge, John Marshall, Aaron Burr, Alexander Hamilton, lawyers of great ability, came into the ranks and performed a leading part in moulding and perfecting our institutions and laws. Still later came in succession, Kent, Story, Pinckney, Tawney, Jackson, Sumner, Calhoun, Benton, Douglas, Clay and Webster, lawyers of supreme sagacity and ability, who in troublesome times debated the great and decisive questions upon which the prosperity and perpetuity of our government depend. Then at the great crisis of our nation appeared the man of destiny, the immortal Lincoln, a lawyer, who, aided by the wise counsel of other eminent lawyers like Chase, Seward, Bates, and Stanton, took us safely through the perils and dangers of a civil war. Then lawyers like Sherman, Thurman, Evarts, Edmunds, Hoar, Field, Phelps and Curtis came upon the scene as guiders of our national life and prosperity. Later, in more modern times (lest invidious distinctions be aroused, I content myself with saying that) many men, strong and great, have from time to time arisen to meet the exigency of the times, among whom stands preeminently in the forefront, at all times, the educated and trained lawyer. So accustomed had we become to the leadership of the lawyer and so difficult is it to depart from a fixed practice, that in the present Congress are found 315 lawyers, constituting two-thirds of the membership of both houses. Substantially, the same proportion of lawyers had characterized the immediately preceding Congress.

Sixteen out of twenty-seven of all our Presidents have been taken from the legal profession, and since Colonial times, the days of our Theocracy, when ministers of the Gospel or other leading citizens, whether lawyers or not, sat in judgment seats, all judges of our courts have been drafted from the legal profession.

So far I have had reference to the national legislative, executive and judicial service, and while I have not made any special examination, I am quite sure that practically the same proportion of lawyers, if not more, have always been found in the several great departments of the state governments. So that it can truly be said lawyers originally constructed the fabric of our federal and state governments, have hitherto always been, and now are, though in a less degree which I will comment on later, the great influencive and controlling forces in our national and state life.

Not only has this been so in the exercise of constructive and governmental functions themselves, but lawyers in the past have been preeminently the leaders of public thought. The people in trust and confidence have looked to them for guidance and direction in their business and also in their political, civil and social affairs.

Into the ranks of this historic body; into the shoes of these illustrious leaders of days gone by, you are soon to come. Unless the established order of things shall be radically changed, which cannot be expected, you are destined not only for service to individual suitors, but for important judicial, legislative and executive duties, state and national.

This hasty review of the past, presenting as it does the wide scope of opportunity, duty, service and influence of the lawyer, makes an attractive and instructing setting for some observations I shall presume to make to you tonight.

To be a lawyer is first to bring yourself into sympathy and working relations with those that have gone before you—the great authors and promoters of our civil and political life and destiny, the wise counsellors and harmonizers of conflicting personal claims and interests; to acquire a proper conception of the dignity and importance of your high calling, and to engage in its service and duty with honesty of purpose and earnest resolve.

Theoretically, and as an attractive generality, you will doubtless agree with me in what I have said so far, but I propose now to go a step farther and make some observations which may not be quite agreeable to you, but the recognition and observance of which I deem to be absolutely essential to an honorable and successful professional career.

The oath required to be taken upon admission to the federal courts, and I presume it is substantially the same in the state courts, is this: "You solemnly swear that you will demean yourself as an attorney and counsellor of this court **uprightly** and according to law and that you will support the Constitution of the United States." This oath, contained in so few words, embraces in a comprehensive and concise way the duties and obligations of an attorney and counsellor at law. The oath plainly indicates that your relation to the Court will be that of one of its officers. Judges, marshals and bailiffs are also officers of the court in their respective spheres, but in no different sense than the attorney and counsellor are. The latter in their particular sphere are as much responsible for the quality of justice administered in the courts as the judge himself is. The lawyer must "demean himself uprightly and according to law." You thus see he is to demean himself not merely "according to law," that is, so not to subject himself to the pains and penalties of of the law merely, but he is to demean himself "uprightly;" that is, honorably, not only according to the dictates of the law, but according to the dictates of absolute right and justice.

An elevated and blameless moral character, therefore, is the first prerequisite to admission to the bar, as it certainly is to efficiency and success in the discharge of the duties of an attorney and counsellor. Without it the lawyer is, and always will be, a dismal failure, whether he be in the office, at the bar or on the bench. Learning in the law is important and necessary. With it, however, but without moral character or a high controlling sense of rectitude and duty, the lawyer will avail but little either for himself or for others.

With both of these qualities and an added element of industry, success is assured.

Not only in the court room, as an officer of the court, is a lawyer to act uprightly, but in the language of the oath, "as counsellor," in his relations to his clients this obligation is imposed upon him. Never was its importance more acute than at the present time. Large business enterprises, involving millions of dollars, economic and social questions affecting the prosperity of all classes, individual rights arising out of or affected by new and hitherto untried legislation and other questions of magnitude and importance are daily rising and pressing for solution. The lawyer of today should, therefore, be a director of things rather than a trier of causes merely. His duties as counsellor out of court are more important to his clients and to the community at large than his duties in actual trials in the courts. Above all things does he owe the obligation of perfect honesty and courage to both client and the public. He can no more honestly advise a client how to evade the law than he can advise him how to violate it. They are the same in essence.

If a lawyer cares only for the money he is to get today, he may possibly acquire a little by advising a client how to accomplish something of doubtful legality or propriety without subjecting him to criminal or civil liability, but this recompense will be slight and precarious. No one, in the end, will condemn him more than the client himself; and the public, to whom he looks for patronage, will despise and avoid him. The responsibility of the lawyer in the way of promoting respect for the law among the people is very great. He can instill in the minds of the people a spirit of respect or disrespect for the law, a spirit of obedience or disobedience to its commands—a feeling of conformity or nonconformity to the spirit of the law. To make my meaning clear, the lawyer should not be the servant, but should be the master of his client. He should give sound advice and require obedience and conformity by a client. Most successful lawyers, I believe, do this, but there are some, who for temporary gain or advantage, give sanction to business projects that are dishonorable and unlawful and assist their clients in their scheming and execution. Many of the unlawful get-rich-quick schemes of recent times, which have wrought widespread trouble and ruin, have received the sanction of lawyers in apparent good standing. I speak this to their shame.

A patent without invention, a mine without mineral, a franchise, lease or contract without value have been capitalized by the fiction of the law which permits money's worth to be taken as money, at grossly false and fictitious value. Advertisements and prospectuses couched in alluring phrase have portrayed the alleged brilliant prospects and promises of the scheme, and at the bottom, in attractive letters, is frequently found a legend something like this: "The legal phases of the enterprise have been under the personal supervision of A. B., one of our ablest and most conservative lawyers."

Trusts, combinations and conspiracies in actual violation of national and state laws have frequently been so veneered by red tape as to seem virtuous and defeat detection.

In ways like these the lawyer actually lends himself to ignoble purposes and base uses. He prostitutes his high calling for pecuniary gain. If, on the other hand, he would courageously and heroically set his foot against the unlawful practices of the present day, as most of them, thank God, do, the result would be soon apparent in a higher regard and deeper respect for the law among the people.

In this connection it will not be unprofitable to dwell a few moments upon certain subjects which have widely attracted public attention in recent times. I have reference to the Interstate Commerce and Anti-Trust Laws of the United States. I wish to make use of them, and particularly of the course of procedure under them, the way they have been treated by the public and by the profession, to illustrate my conception of the duty and responsibility of the lawyer.

Prior to 1887, the date of the original Interstate Commerce Act, the principles of the common law with respect to monopoly and discrimination were the only guides to business conduct on those subjects. The admonitions of the common law were gentle, attended with no harsh, severe or penal consequences. They were, nevertheless, well understood by the profession. It was as unlawful then to monopolize trade in any given department as it is today. It was as unlawful for common carriers to discriminate in favor of one shipper against another in rates of freight as it now is, but the consequences of doing so were not serious. A civil action for redress was practically the only remedy and this was so uncommon as to be little feared by any offenders. The lawyers, however, knew that those practices were unlawful, contrary to public policy and ought not to have been practiced.

In 1887 the first Interstate Commerce Act was passed by Congress. It forbade, in clear and definite terms, any and all discriminations in favor of one shipper over and above the rate others were compelled to pay and provided certain more effective remedies than had before that time existed for its infraction. In this way the lawyers were not only reminded of the common law principles which had hitherto existed as their guides, but their action was called sharply to the imperative requirements of the statutory law. Later, in 1890, Congress passed the Sherman Anti-Trust Law denouncing combinations in the nature of trusts and monopolies and conferring ample power upon the courts of equity to suppress them.

By this act the lawyer, the traditional guardian of our liberties and the people's rights, the man to whom the public looked for the enforcement of its laws and whose oath of office required him to perform the duties uprightly and according to law, was again sharply commanded to perform his duty.

Yet notwithstanding these things, it is a notorious fact that combinations in the nature of trusts, monopolies, rebates on freight rates, schemes and devices of all sorts, intended and adapted to circumvent these laws, throve as they never had thrived before. The laws were openly defied. Large combinations became larger. Monopolies increased, discrimination and rebates were openly granted. From 1890 to 1903 there seemed to be no check upon them. Many lawyers were engaged in devising schemes to respect the letter and ignore the spirit of the laws. The ablest in the land were engaged by the powerful financial interests. They created the trusts. They consented to the monopolies and by their advice and direction violations of the spirt and meaning of the laws, if not their letter, were of frequent occurrence. In 1903, however, forbearance ceased to be a virtue. In that year the famous Elkins Amendment to the Interstate Commerce Act was passed by Congress. It aimed prominently to suppress the then most prevalent practice of allowing rebates by common carriers to favored shippers. It was not very severe in the way of penalties for its violations, but it was born of a stern determination to suppress the practice. It was reinforced in 1906 by the Hepburn Act and again in 1910 by the well-known Administration Act of that year. During these later years as the legislative department of the government put on activity to prevent rebates and discriminations in the nature of trusts and monopolies, the judicial department zealously began prosecutions for such violations. As you all know, drastic measures have been resorted to. Railroad companies and other corporations engaged in interstate commerce, which before that time had openly disregarded the law, at least concerning rebates, have been driven to bay. Instead of repenting in sackcloth and ashes as they should have done, and given assurance of respect and obedience to the law in the future, they declaim vociferously against destruction of business and inveigh against legislation which they call harsh and destructive. In other words, they have not yielded themselves to respect for the law. If they try to conform to its letter they do not recognize or respond to the spirit and essential meaning of the law.

But that recognition must and will come. Unless it does, the institutions of our country secured by patriotic self-denial and sacrifice will be seriously imperiled if not destroyed.

Unless there be a cheerful obedience to the law, a willing submission to its essential and broad requirements on the part of the intelligent business interests of the country, we cannot reasonably expect such obedience and respect on the part of those less intelligent. I know of no more effective instruction in misrule, nothing so inevitably tending to anarchy, as the object lesson of the past twenty years afforded by some of our business men.

Now, how has this come to pass? I do not believe it results from an intentional disobedience of the law, or from a spirit of determined defiance of the law, but I rather believe it comes from a condition of mental and moral indifference. The public conscience is at a low stage. The desire for money-getting has taken possession of men and in its gratification, the means have not been scrupulously considered. The end to be accomplished has dulled the moral sense and justified most any means for reaching it.

That I may not be misunderstood, I wish to say that I am not condemning business itself. Far from it. Great success in business is admirable if accomplished by fair, honest and lawful means. Large accumulations by one man are not criminal. They bespeak for him the possession of exceptional qualities of head and heart. Monopoly does not consist merely in large accumulations. A man is entitled to all he can honestly make. It is large accumulations of money by dishonest and unlawful means that constitute that monopoly which is condemned by law.

The responsibility for this dull conscience among business men, this greediness for money which has unhorsed the man and saddled the miser, rests, in my opinion, not solely upon the man of business. It rests equally upon the lawyers who are his professional advisers. The latter have become subservient when they should have been masters. They have become tolerant of unlawful practices, to accomodate their clients. They have sought loopholes of exit from the manifest requirements of the law, when they should have sought its fair and reasonable interpretation and insisted upon conformity to it. As a result they are now suffering in lost influence and prestige, and their clients are suffering from what they are pleased to call drastic legislation and bitter prosecutions, both civil and criminal.

In my opinion, however, the experiences of the last twenty years have not been in vain. A better time is coming when all, taught by sad experience though they may have been, will learn respect for the law in its essence and true meaning, and will observe genuine obedience to its dictates. At any rate, they will learn, I am sure, that honesty is the best policy.

By conduct like that which I have just adverted to, on the part of the lawyers who have been called to advise in large matters, and as a result of the general commercializing tendency, the profession has lost much of its ancient prestige. The people are too prone to let exceptional acts of lawyers handling large and conspicuous transactions characterize the entire profession, and I fear they are now in these days blaming the profession as a whole for what is taught and practiced by the few only.

The names of eminent statesmen, authors, artists and particularly business men are on the tongues of the people. Formerly the names of the great lawyers like Webster, Clay, Marshall, Edmunds, Evarts, Choate and others were daily mentioned and much revered. The ideal lawyer doubtless exists today as heretofore, but the public no longer appreciates him as the great influencive force—the leading spirit of the day.

Formerly the people looked to him for advice and direction. He was the delegate to conventions civil, religious and political; chairman of meetings, and the promoter-general of the people's interests. He held a unique position. He was sought for because of his knowledge, wisdom and sagacity. Now, instead of the people seeking him, he seeks them. His call to office, instead of being the spontaneous expression of the people's wish, usually is an extravagant laudation of his own merits prepared by himself or some confidential friend. While he frequently gets there, it is not generally because of his own superior merit or greater acceptability; not because he is in fact the people's idol, but because of his personal solicitation and importunity, and often because of promises of future official favors if he shall succeed. The profession, as a whole, has lost its ancient prestige. Lawyers seem to have lost love for her. It is not uncommon to witness a lawyer of eminent and commanding ability and influence leaving the ranks of his profession for the presidency of a bank, a railroad or other large corporate enterprise. Instead of acquiring broad culture in the law and kindred subjects requisite for leadership, he fits himself for business, and even if he stays in the profession, he frequently accepts employment by some powerful interest which takes all his time and attention. He becomes specialized exactly as business has become specialized.

So true is this that Dr. Woodrow Wilson, recent president of Princeton University, now Governor-elect of New Jersey, a great observer, and an acknowledged student and philosopher of the times, recently exclaimed: "Lawyers are not now regarded as the mediators of progress. * * * Look what legal questions are to be settled, how stupendous they are, how far-reaching, and how impossible it will be to settle them without the advice of learned and experienced lawyers! The country must find lawyers of the right sort, and of the old spirit to advise it, or it must stumble through a very chaos of blind experiment. It never needed lawyers who are statesmen more than it needs them now, needs them in its courts, in its legislatures, in its seats of executive authority—lawyers who can think in the terms of society itself, mediate between interests, accommodate right to right, establish equity, and bring the peace that will come with genuine and hearty co-operation, and will come in no other way."

The question is often asked, and frequently debated, whether a lawyer may take a case which he knows is without merit. To this question, so far as the **prosecution** of a suit is concerned, there can be but one answer. Of course, he cannot. To do so would not only encourage the client in the perpetration of a wrong, involve himself in an immoral and unethical transaction, but would necessarily involve the practice of an imposition and fraud upon the court of which he is a sworn officer. His function as a counselor here comes into action. His duty, when such a case is presented to him, is clear. He should advise his client that he has no case, charge him a reasonable fee for the service and retire from further participation in it. This will save the client the trouble and expense of protracted and futile litigation, preserve his own honor and self-respect and defend the court, of which he is an officer, from the proposed imposition. No high-minded and conscientious lawyer can do otherwise. To proceed with such a case would involve an attempt to win a case by tricks of practice or disclose a willingness to manufacture, distort or suppress facts and deceive the court. In either way he would lend himself to a dishonorable, unlawful and criminal project, destructive of his own self-respect and calculated to bring himself into infamy and disgrace. There are, however, cases which are not definitely without merit, or bad ones, about which differences of opinion may exist as to their merits, which a lawyer may engage in and present to the court for its determination even though his private opinion may be adverse to recovery. This is often true where a right or a principle is to be established. But this is quite different from the cases just considered which the lawyer knows to be bad.

Should he undertake the defense of a case which he knows is without merit? If it is a civil case for reasons already averted to he should not. His sole relation to it should be that of counselor to faithfully and honestly advise his client as to him seems right. If it is a criminal case the answer may be somewhat different. Even in this his advice to his client should in all cases be honest, and if he be guilty the best advice would be for him to plead guilty and submit himself to the judgment of the court. But, by reason of the fact that there are frequently several degrees of the same offense and a graduation of punishment dependent upon the intent with which it is committed, an inquiry into all the facts and circumstances with the view of ascertaining that intent, is entirely permissible, and employment to defend a person charged with a crime can, to this extent at least, be always ac-accepted. But no worthy lawyer will prostitute his high calling to the deliberate purpose of acquitting him if he knows him to be guilty.

The principle of fidelity of a lawyer to his client, which is often invoked to justify him in the prosecution or defense of an unrighteous cause, is frequently made to do shameful service. There is no loftier or nobler principle than this when properly applied. Fidelity to a client after you shall have engaged in his service is imperative. It is born of a high sense of duty and obligation. It requires the lawyer to strictly observe his client's confidence and perform faithfully, loyal and zealous service in his behalf. It, however, can never be invoked to require employment at the start. The confidential relation out of which springs the obligation of fidelity has not then been established. The question of employment must always be left to a lawyer's own deliberate choice and conscience. Neither can it be invoked to require or justify a resort to perjury or subornation of perjury or any other criminal, fraudulent or dishonorable conduct in the promotion of his client's welfare or interests. Sharp practice, deception, graft, fraud, perjury, are each and all the tools of the pettifogger and shyster. Of course, I need not, before this intelligent and right-minded audience, denounce the shyster or trickster in the law. They frequently, and regretfully, are made to represent the profession in low comedy and oftentimes in higher histrionic performances, but I protest against that misrepresentation—that distortion of the truth and that great slander upon a noble profession. The tricks of the imposter are never practiced by the real lawyer. He has no such tools in his box. Notwithstanding these most obvious limitations upon the lawyer's sphere of action, there is a wide legitimate and honorable field of operation for him. The best, well-trained and conscientious lawyer will surely be sought for and employed. Now and then a great civil case arises in court which calls for the best service of the best man. Not so much, however, for his eloquence, as for his deep learning, his patient research, his simple and effective presentation of the law and facts of the case. Now and then a great criminal case arises which calls for a man of somewhat different qualities; now and then a case either civil or criminal, of ordinary consequence and importance only arises which calls for the best service a true and faithful attorney can render for his client. But after all, the great demand for the lawyer of today is as counselor in the varied and complex affairs of life. In this sphere his learning and talents can be of the greatest public and private use. If the lawyers of this country would only avail themselves of their opportunities they could give tone and direction to social and business life, and acquire fame and renown for themselves. Let the lawyer get into the habit of saying "no" instead of "yes." Let him have convictions born of law-abiding and law-enforcing disposition and have the courage to express them and enforce them on all appropriate occasions, and he will again be found at the head and front of our civil, social and political life as his forebears were. The general tone of business will be improved and a competency for himself and those dependent upon him will surely be acquired.

But I am asked if this is not too visionary and ideal for practical purposes; if it does not lose sight of the admitted fact that a vocation is primarily and necessarily for the purpose of making a living for one's self and those dependent upon him.

Of course, a lawyer cannot live on ethics or honors alone. He must have a reasonable compensation for his services. In my opinion the better the quality of the service, in all cases, the greater should be the pecuniary compensation for it. The emoluments and rewards of professional life are necessarily of prime importance to every lawyer. He need not disdain honorable employment in any matter, however small, or in any court, however humble. In services like these many a beginner has laid the foundation for a successful career, but whatever be the service or in whatever court it may be undertaken, it must be honest, zealous and courageous. Business men as a rule are honest. They expect nothing else of a lawyer than honest service, dependent upon the facts of the case as they may appear. They commend a lawyer for these qualities and quickly recognize that they are the only ones worth having, or worth paying for. They despise tricks and sharp practice, and when discovered, refuse to patronize their possessors. Character, learning, courage, fidelity, industry always have won and always will win, and their pecuniary compensations in the long run will far outweigh any temporary advantage which can come from the best laid trick a shyster can devise.

Now, how is the student of law to equip himself for this high calling, this exalted service, this service profitable to himself and at the same time beneficial to the public?

These questions, right here in this law school you are, in my opinion, answering in the only rational and effective manner. Here you are in an atmosphere of pure learning. In a community of professors and teachers who draw their inspiration from the source of all knowledge, goodness and power, and who are laboriously and faithfully striving to impress upon you the great fundamental truths of law and justice.

Any suggestion I can make will add little if any to the teaching which you are constantly receiving; but if I may presume so far I would like to suggest that you make no haste in your preparation work. Take all necessary time so that the great underlying principles of the law which are being daily taught you may thoroughly permeate your intellect and judgment. Get familiar not only with the text of the rule, but with the reason of it. The old maxim "**qui haeret in litera haeret in cortice**" is as important for you to recognize in your preparatory period as it is for judges to recognize in the interpretation of laws. Reflect upon and ponder over the great principles till they are yours and do not confine yourself to the reading of law books only. Read broadly and widely not only from the sages of the law, but on any subject of human knowledge so far as you may. It will all aid you in your future work. In these days of wonderful things when forces hitherto hidden and mysterious are being harnessed to do the bidding of man in daily business transactions, a lawyer must, if he would attain a great success, become familiar with them or at least have such an understanding of them as will enable him to appreciate their significance and make application of them as occasion may require.

In these days of new thought, new economics, new forces, new social, political and religious theories, how pitiable is the plight of one who aspires to advise and lead men and does not have an enlightened general understanding of these things! Lay broad, therefore, the foundations of your wisdom and learning that they may be the quicker recognized by your expected clients and avail you most effectively when discovered.

From what I have now said it is apparent there are two kinds of lawyers (I do not classify the shyster or pettifogger as any kind of a lawyer, and therefore pass him by). The one is an independent, masterful, courageous, honest leader of men and of public thought. A man who advises his clients and tries his causes in the fear of the law and tolerates neither evasion nor subterfuge, the kind which has brought honor and distinction to the profession and fame and renown to the individual. The other is the astute organizer, the servant rather than the master of his client, the apologizer for the wrong instead of champion for the right.

The one is the ideal lawyer of the old time of which, I am pleased to testify, we still have many. The other is a new creation of modern times, the commercialized specialist brought into existence and developed to a high state of efficiency by the necessities of our modern business. The honors of the profession, with a reasonable competence, belongs, as a rule, to the first class. The second class may for a time reap a greater pecuniary reward, but their position is not comparable to his who practices the law in spirit as well as letter and constantly maintains the time-honored standards of the noble profession to which we belong.

Printed by Libri Plureos GmbH in Hamburg, Germany